Half-Life

poems

Jane Ann Fuller

Sheila-Na-Gig Editions

Volume 9

ISBN: 978-1-7354002-4-2
Library of Congress Control Number: 2021938749

Published by Sheila-Na-Gig Editions
Russell, KY
Hayley Mitchell Haugen, Editor
www.sheilanagigblog.com

To Jesse, Molly, and Finn

For their father

"A widow trains her body to hear grace notes. Fatigue. Duration. When solace seems far off, she offers *water bending light*. Unflinching poems walk readers through *bones in a furnace* to offer forgiveness. Feel *birds sift through you*, as you meet her Icarus. *Half-Life* enters family trauma, teaching flight and nesting. Fuller rends hearts then mends them. With exquisite locution, with keen listening, she paints a *constellation where we keep our better selves*. We recognize her landscape of grief in ourselves."

—Lori Anderson Moseman, Y *(The Operating System)*

"As readers of Fuller's *Half-Life*, we can only marvel at the quest to understand human nature in her unflinching study of art and the natural world. The act of processing tragedy by analysis cannot be mistaken for indifference; in fact, it's heartbreaking. The narrator has learned that in order to get on with the often dark business of living, one simply must persist. As survivors, we are returned to our own imaginations, and if we are as fortunate as Fuller's narrator, we find ourselves in the presence of the sublime: *We can only imagine what you wanted, what you saw of us on the ground, waving frantically, happy at first you were flying, then swimming out to find you in the brilliant surf.*"

— Deni Naffziger, *Desire to Stay*, nominated for the Weatherford Award

"Jane Ann Fuller takes on grief like a bird about to collide with herself on window glass. Because she also sees through to something else. To Icarus: ... *feathers, you oil them with hope.* . . Extraordinary poetry, hard, reflexive truth: *And you, in your willingness to surrender / your life, might appreciate my grieving /*

now that I have paid attention, / now that I know it's not love you were after, / but order. Something manageable. / Something of another world."

— Paul Nelson, author of *Learning to Miss*

"*Half-Life* takes us to the darkest of places by way of Bruegel, whose *Massacre of the Innocents* was painted over, softening the siege to a pillage: *The limbs of speared infants piled, painted over as mashed bushels of fruit…* These poems originate in pain, yet they radiate light through their intense music and color. Children grow up in the shadow cast by their father's absence, his decision to leave. His dead star still shines at the poet through the blackness of space. There is something to be said for what Frost called *being acquainted with the night*. However harrowing the questions, Fuller asks them with a rare and original grace."

—Hillary Sideris, *Animals in English, Poems after Temple Grandin*

ACKNOWLEDGMENTS

Gratitude to the editors of these journals in which some of these poems appeared in slightly different form.

All We Know of Pleasure: Poetic Erotica By Women: "Everything Depends Upon"

Atticus Review: "Exchange Of Stars"

B O D Y: "Flashpoint," "Suicides"

Fifth Wednesday: "Postmodern Woman Bathing"

Grist: "Did Anyone Think To Ask The Horse?"

JMWW: "Because One Death Belongs To Us All," "Calendula," "Potamophobia," and "Reading By Streetlamp On Governor Ave."

Kaimana: "The Onion," "What They Don't Know"

Northern Appalachia Review: "Leaving The Old House," "Shame"

Pine Mountain Sand and Gravel: "According To The Old Farmer's Almanac, January 13, 2003, is Plough Monday"

Project Hope: "Birdhouse Gourds"

Pudding Magazine: "Wanting You"

Rise Up Review: "The Value Of A Woman"

Shenandoah: "Conversation With Two-Time Mid-American Conference Relief Pitcher Douglas Dean Stackhouse On Winning, Losing, And Learning To Fiddle," awarded the 2015 James Boatwright III Poetry Prize, and "Recovery"

Steinbeck Now: "At The Feeder, Early November," "Chickadee" published as "Bird," and "How To Understand Desire For An Elsewhere"

Still: The Journal: "Winter Wheat"

Sugar House Review: "Landscape, With Family"

The American Journal of Poetry: "Rigor"

The Ekphrsatic Review: "Humanities 101"

The MacGuffin: "Camellia," "Late"

The Pikeville Review: "Mythology"

Waccamaw: "Sitting Centerfield On The Night Game Of Your Suicide"

CONTENTS

1.

2.

1

But often the shadow seems more real than the body.

– Thomas Transtromer

HALF-LIFE

After authorities find the body of a man
in the woods off Jake Tom Road

What's left of your tracks
is lit by lilies, orange and wild,
as if to say why
you chose this path
from the truck you left idling,
as if you'd be right back,
just stepped off to piss
or pick a handful for a window jar.

You left us to imagine
how light splintered the hawthorn,
how your boots cracked acorns like gunfire,
bones in a furnace, an idea clicking finally into place:

The living boast.
What do they know?

EXCHANGE OF STARS

Now say *i-so-LAY-ted* with the Scottish researcher's elongated accent,
as she explains on NPR the needle exchange program
piloting in Turner, Indiana, and how the addict need not be

laid out like the body whose rigor-mortised fist
clutches the shoestring or the sister's scarf.

Then *re-COV-ray,* the *cov* long and flat, a country of its own,
barren of fleshiness, population nearing zero—
say it, like that, with the near-brogue.

Now say it like an *Appalatchin,* a user, truly
assolated: stress on the first
short *a* as in *ass* and *apple* and
accident. Know that what it sounds like
may not be what it is—

so much more than the formal note of his voice
when the deputy calls you around the building
to tell you what you already know, your own name
dead on his tongue already having
splayed you and since you can't look at him, your mind goes
to *fatigue*—how the French say It.
What a gorgeous word
and what it must feel like to die

as you shoot up, your nerves melting into liquid gold,

your pinhole pupils still holding the cosmos—

the exchange of stars

those of us left to count

down toward—just junk—

dead but still glimmering

on the blackest heaven.

Recovery

to Jesse

Better a small, wild death—
the doe and perhaps a trailing pair of fawns—

than your Ford flipped into the Hocking
where Scott's Creek meets the train yard.

In this place it makes sense
not to swerve when the deer leap for Lodi

or fields of hog corn. Remember
just north of Phoenix when you stopped to help

the blue pickup idling on the shoulder,
the man with his buck knife

waiting there for anyone? It happened
to be you who knelt with the doe,

pulled her weight, as he coached you,
into your own. You say her black eyes

burned into you and then went dead,
two spent bulbs. You held on to them

as long as reason would allow.
You say helping her through seemed

spiritual, visceral as any remembering,
now that you've felt in her weight

the absence of expectation.
What it is to stop wanting.

How To Understand Desire For An Elsewhere

On the road between my house and hers
a woman walks her lot: children,
two on scooters, one on foot,
and their dog, a big male Airedale.

Who knows where her husband is, probably inside
watching other men beat around a ball,
driving one toward a hoop, or hitting
another into a small, perfect hole.

I'm no better. I'm watching from the window
imagining you not watching anything,
nor walking, just floating around like an idea
of somewhere else. I'm pretty certain

elsewhere is measured by the sanity of men
I would not recognize, alone in their madrigal,
eternal summers. But here, nightfall works
this cobalt blue into my memory

of a Parrish painting I'd inhabit
just to watch me watch myself cry.
And you, in your willingness to surrender
your life, might appreciate my grieving

now that I have paid attention,

now that I know it's not love you were after,

but order. Something manageable.

Something of another world.

SUBLIME ICARUS

> *...the sun shone*
> *As it had to on the white legs disappearing into the green*
> *Water...*
> —W. H. Auden, "Musée des Beaux Arts"

When you chose to die, you chose
duration, a pocket of memory
to guide us because nothing else
you could think of
was anything like this
kind of forgiveness
we're giving you now.

Still, in the morning, when the air is fresh
and the sun's cloak catches
on its own useless fingers,
you descend. We wait
by the window and listen for the first
birds of June to unfasten your wings.

We want to hear it like the blast of a shotgun,
the weather you swallowed, as falling,
your body gave up all it had to remind us
to listen. We are listening. We have not heard
any remarkable words. Nor birds.

Let the sun, observing the flight of a small boy,

transport him. Not to his death, but beyond

toward the blue confession of falling

where he finds himself freer than his father,

out of time, fleshy as time may seem, and forgiven.

Because One Death Belongs To Us All

in this small Appalachian town,
we prefer metaphor: suicide becomes love;
a bullet ricochets; and even after the death of reason
something lives where the impression of a body
that could have been sleeping, the grass,
pressed down, springs into commitment:

Whatever else happens in the story,
buckled roots of oak, horn-white, and
bees drowning in sour mash,

entire bridges of stone, hand-carved
and large as church foundations
collapse where Scott's Creek inseminates The Hocking.
And as if riding a rail car west to the yard,
closed and quaint with local history,
someone will get it right,
why someone else chose to leave us.

And drunk, how we gesture understanding:
You can't see what disappears, but after a death,
you feel the birds sift through you.

CHICKADEE

One of them is dead beneath the window.
The others, blind to him, flit to seed,
their cumulative weight making the feeder swing
as the light shifts to contain it.

The bird has been there for days
on its back, its body gray and downy,
its black mask muffled by the other black mask.
Its eyes are half-slits, head turned away,

beak ajar like the blades of scissors
I might take from my drawer. A smudge of red
makes us curious, the dog scratching to go out.
I will wait until she sleeps on the rug.

I will probably not look long at the small
body, beautiful still. The tail feathers
will make an easy handle
for hitching into the woods.

Reflection

It is natural for the robin
to slam into glass
that gives back the enemy

so completely. I watch her
watch the other bird
who would steal into her nest,

her plans all but hatched.
It is natural to fear
what is thrown back—

how many times?
All morning long. I called to her
with her own song.

At dusk we tried to separate
ourselves from knowing,
but we lay her down

in tall grasses, crooked,
her breast smudged,
still warm with recognition.

Mythology

Trouble is, your wings fit you
like a cage fits a bird,

just the right size for pacing
the finite. And those feathers,

you oil them with hope,
so that when the light blinds us,

you see a door suddenly ajar.
When you squeeze through,

it seems logical
to claim your way out:

you could pass for a gannet
dive-bombing sardines.

You blend into the frenzy
of black-tipped pitch,

white-winged yaw.
The beauty muffles the horror.

Humanities 101

The slaughtered babies [of Pieter Bruegel the Elder's original]
were painted over with details such as bundles, food and animals so that,
instead of a massacre, it appeared to be a more general scene of plunder.
—On *Massacre of the Innocents*

Soldiers piss against a wall. Icicles hang,
will never fall, though we will them to impale

the German mercenary who scales a barrel
to enter the window of a fraulein's house.

What he will ruin will remain
mystery, even today. Something original,

changed, still flames in your great-great-great
grandmother's bed, this stein of mead, the pewter

taste of blood; today on College Green
the bell tower's carillon sounds

like air raid sirens in Kabul to a young man
next to me who doesn't speak but stays behind

his medicated smile. Professor plays
"A Love Supreme," and other twentieth-century

diatonic jazz. What lies beneath eventually
bleeds. The limbs of speared infants piled,

painted over as mashed bushels of fruit,
geese you find alive and white as the down

of a baby, drawn, in this 1988 conservation
of Bruegel's *Massacre of the Innocents.*

Today, as if for the first time, I see her,
the daughter, slight as a thorn that works its way

to the surface. She reaches for her mother.
Like the others she will be raped, quartered,

stacked against the lean-to like wood.

The Value Of A Woman

Flying birds find something, sitting birds only find death.
I have found both women and churches.
— Beggar, *Virgin Spring*

If you don't want to know the value of a girl
delivering candles to church
don't watch *Virgin Spring*.
Maybe hang a bird feeder, instead,
with your daughter home on spring break—
Teach her thistle brings them around, but oiled
sunflower seeds make them stay, chickadees
in their little black masks.

Tell her the birds will come.
Think to yourself: *It happened. A girl was raped*
and murdered. At least you weren't
murdered.

Don't ask her,
What did they do to you?

Instead, finish the housework and remember:
residue of bird on the window and
a fool's expectation both
cling, like all these power lines clinging to the sky and

cinching what was to what is—her body before
and after.

Accept, eventually,
or disappear from her life, entirely,
forever.

Live on the ridges under the spring sky in Hocking County,
where anything is possible. Birds return
to the feeder for the sunflower
we offer without thinking. Out of habit
or instinct, the birds return.

Remember, they left her on the hillside,
her lips kissing the April grass.
Tell your daughter exactly how
she will survive. Tell her,

You will become a woman.
That's how.

DID ANYONE THINK TO ASK THE HORSE?

What if I told you, daughter, you scream like an animal,
half wild, half domesticated, your naked haunches slick
with sweat and blood, and that it's okay to forgive yourself
for being unconscious on the night you were drugged
and raped, the night you narrowly escaped
—narrowly—
that there's nothing to forgive?

Would you believe me?
If not this, then what would you believe?

What if I told you that every night, faceless,
you star in my dreams, a survivor,
caught beneath the weight of a dark horse
that's fallen on the road, what has tried
to find its way inside you—
twice, three times your size.

I see that he did not succeed.
I see, but what if I say
nothing? What if we shared this
knowledge, peripherally?

What if some master artist painted you
as a mashed bushel of fruit, your pale legs

thrashing like corn stalks?

Where will you sleep?

Will the horse, who by now is every man
you've ever trusted, scratch his innocent
behind on a tree? What if the tree
is in a painting no one will discuss?
What if the tree were made of paper,
something we could fold
into meaning, an origami?

What if the man who rode in on the horse
is skewering a woman behind the brick
and mortar house so we cannot see?

If the plowed rows are tinctured
with pinkish, sanguine light;
if the horse retires to his stall after dark,
whether or not he sleeps, the buzzing of a fly
making him twitch with no remorse;
and if the moon's face is blank
as a pickerel's, who will remember?

The Torturer's Horse

> *Where the dogs go on with their doggy life and the torturer's horse*
> *Scratches its innocent behind on a tree.*
> —W. H. Auden, "Musée des Beaux Arts"

Imagine how spent the animal
returning from his master's work,
haunches slick as faceless night,
eyes wide as Asia, west, to Africa,
between, furrowed India and the Arabian Sea.

What have they seen in that peripheral chance:
the pale arms of a girl, thrashing,
her waist a dune on which depravity will sleep,
her soul like milkweed popping
its perfectly wandering seed.
Life behind him simply
not happening—the plowed rows
tinctured with pinkish light.

He retires to the stall, credulous,
and sleeps or doesn't sleep,
the moon blank as the pickerel sky,
his mind trained to believe suffering
is nothing, really—a new sunrise blooming,
perhaps, and he shudders at the buzzing of a fly.

You masters who made me believe

his illuminating gait, his huge ass

backing into the shaggy bark of a paper tree,

I might curse you if I didn't know better:

no matter how you paint it,

that mangle of male children

becomes a mashed bushel of fruit,

a daughter meaningless as wood,

the horse fated to participate

again found innocent.

Hunger

What she didn't know
he'd teach her—

how to weight the trap
with the animal, sinking in the pond,
wild, thieving,
as hard to carry as the concrete Buddha
she'd bought for the perennial bed.

To catch and release
is not allowed.

It occurs to me her innocence
turned like a cheek turns
in denial
the moment he hit her. Suddenly

this thing had everything to do
with everything else.

Holding firm
when vermin come
to raid the compost pile, eat scraps set out for cats
we've nearly tamed, she's not afraid

to act. It's required
to keep the population down.

He loved her so he hit her so he said,
It's what you want,
to know how much,
and for how long.

I understand her willingness
to try the tangled logic on for size.
We want, as women often do,
to know we have the guts to hold our own
in concert with the mad.

He was an animal
caught in a trap.
Pacing.
Thumbing the latch.

They lumber through the dark,
wise or dumb, purposeful,
or simply hungry. Following their noses,
their rumbling insides,
insignificant to the world in its grand,
patriarchal scheme. Let them play,
some of you think. Let them be.

Her cheek burns
from the cold this November
without stars to guide her, just
memory of
meeting him for the first time
beneath the pines.

The stars were dark
the clouds a bruise across the sky.
What she didn't know
he'd teach her
to help him weight the trap with a raccoon
whose eyes were black
whose nervous thumbs were her thumbs
traveling her clasps.

They sink fast. Have-a-harts' whose
tiniest latch keeps them caught.

Together, we watch
the breathing stop. We haul the trap
and leave the carcass to the field.

Crows arrange themselves
like suitors on the lawn.

LANDSCAPE, WITH FAMILY

Let your eyes go to her first
since she's the beauty
of the daughters, her brown hair
taken with gray, her blue eyes
squinting in dusk's favored light.

The old man's smile rushes
its banks, takes you
suddenly. Beware his nose
like the bit of an axe
sharp and requiring. A bird

alighting on her shoulder,
his hand spreads
its wings. The field has grown
into a sea of dry flame
in which to stand waist high

with those who remain.
Behind them, the shade
of a farm house fades
among trees; hills roll toward
a sky whited out.

Winter Wheat

1.

I drive my daughter east and south
beside sandstone cliffs where
workers planted dynamite
then scrub pines that grow horizontal
now, as if they float,
to keep the cutout from eroding.

As we enter Athens County
(whose university sits like an egg
in an open field) my thoughts
form with girls who travel there.
And my daughter? We both know

men who rape girls
live there. Men
who hold a kind of power and choose
not to prosecute the men who rape
girls work there.
Men also exist
who do not know because the girl
(and her mother)
never told them,
(if the girl or if the girl's mother had told them,

there would be more murder in this world.)

2.

In the open cup
of hair and grass
fledglings wait for her
white hips, blue wings and
four-pronged claws
that hop the trunk
upside down,
resistant
to weather and competing birds,
to feed them. Common as she is, this American
Sparrow, she helps us
imagine a watchful god.

3.

Why do they plant in December,
the farmers, in blue, shifting light?
This year they had to harvest winter wheat
and plant it twice. Now,
birds flock to the harrowed fields.

(I don't know anything about planting.
I know about escaping the rule of light.)

We drive through fields of bronze, pools of sadness,
opening the locks.

4.

Coveries and *locutions* are beautiful words.
Do you know them?

A mother and her daughter find
a nuthatch nest. In a pine whose flickering light
and needles coax them.

Blurred like the background
of a photograph is this
phantom pain.

Mother and daughter watch while juncos and tit mice
fill their cheeks at the hanging feeder.
She is not in the photograph
except to be the photographer's tool.
You can't make her out
among the hemlock.

Rigor

to a suicide

1. Sanibel Heat

The wind resurrects
embers as daylight stars,
scatters what we feed to fire
—carambola, lychee nut
grief-heavy starfruit branches.

I never imagined
(my jaw set) (your hazel eyes)
you'd turn from this work
but how foolish we look
raking the dead

eucalyptus leaves into this
coral ring of fire
(as in the crematorium
you might have sat straight up
in revelatory heat.) Your heart last to burn.

2. Rigor

When they handed me the box of you,
it was smaller than I had imagined.
Inside, your ashes wrapped in plastic.
Above us squirrels
quarreled in a shared highway of trees,
the weight of you
a cool relief, but now
I wake mid-dream,
the animal smell, familiar
on our sheets, the sweat of late September
when I chose to move the *wedding veil*.

Your eyes were turtles—
green with flecks of gold,
your freckled shoulders bared,
and then—your sunken chest
when rigor set (they let me see)

but not your head
gathered in a towel
where the bullet slept, and
wilting steel-toed boots
splattered with cement
they wouldn't let me keep.

3. The Lucky Ones

I've never been good with animals
so when you died, your sister took the rabbit.

I tried to save some strange small lives
from parasites that left their hind legs skating out.

I buried them where the ground was right.
I used slants of evening light to light my cigarette,

leaned toward the flame and singed my hair
and jerked the cage to make them stop

—the budgies "tssssk."
It's spring: they are making love.

Beta fish I separate in mason jars
beneath the window on this other world

sleep among the plastic grass all day.

Rock House

A tunnel-like corridor situated midway up a 150-foot cliff
of Blackhand sandstone in Hocking Hills State Park.

Sometimes they're so brave I want to shake them,

the children, running toward the edge,

wrestling over it, as if plunging

seventy-five feet directly down

would simply be cartoonish, a waterfall fall.

My heart stops. I stop

dead in my tracks and wait for them

to follow their other instinct,

the one that preserves them,

that leads them back to my side

as I wind back down the trail

over the weathered sandstone steps

and up again to the safety

and boredom of the car.

But are they brave,

or are they simply drawn,

equilibrium strung,

toward their father, gone

helmet-less without them?

He gave them a lesson early on—

the worst is something

they will never have to imagine,

which gives them the right

to run toward the opening of the cave

if just for the view,

if just to look down on

what could kill them.

What They Don't Know

is courage
comes packaged as grief.
Paper left to mildew on the stoop,
one of many versions of the story.
Some of us drive to another county
where the glacier stopped
two hundred million years ago
to find round stones for a pond we've dug
for goldfish we've seen grow as large
as their container will allow. Like a room
filling with smoke, the longer we sit here
and listen to all the necessary stories.
Sometimes I think of you as one of us
sitting in the back since you were once
so tall, your presence made the doorway
seem a window, the rest of us birds
who might fly through if you'd just
step aside, your story perfect as the one
that's found its ending.

2

To be wild means nothing you do or have done

needs to be explained.

– Stephen Dunn

LOCUTIONS

words from the supernatural that enter the mind spontaneously,
translated into your own language and offering heavenly consolation.

These crows
wake me every morning in July,
and in August, neighbors' little dogs
yap as if tethered to old women in a queue.

Dusk becomes the death
whose spirit clings.
Tree-frogs surge: *hurry*
now, come here.

When you left,
dishes piled, a fleet
of warships in the sink,
the furnace filter going gray,

I sat in the bamboo,
beneath remarkable stars.
I should tell you,
in this half-life other-world
rain falls into September—
much of it lost to puddles on the lawn—

why you cannot hear me
in this quiet blunder.
You are with the words
I did not choose. Forgive me.
I chose wrong.

Magnolia

And behind you, or the thought of you,
bamboo grows brown and green by turns,

hiding things or losing them: a child
or one pink winter glove.

Behind the barn the redbud rots,
the limb we sat on broken off.

You'll find a plague of onion grass;
one spindly spiderwort

your mother has the wherewithal to love.
Yellow tulips knuckle deep.

Goldfish thrive beneath the ice
of my makeshift pond,

one black as sleep, one gold.

Where Nothing You Do Needs To Be Explained

This is where the gun you tossed
sank for everyone you ever loved

where stones you carry in your pockets
on your chest for everyone who couldn't act

and ghosts
guilty of their hunger can't rest

raid your garden patch and work
the locks of your sunken traps.

Where solace is cast
and lost. Where you wait at dusk

with day-old bread and toss it out
where water bends the light.

SHAME

I just don't see the shame in loving what you've got, say,

a small pond as opposed to an ocean,

not even half an acre,

because loving a small pond, by default, is like loving

the small town I come from. Isn't love a metaphor

for all the excuses I have ever made for staying

where I'm most alive,

even if that means I don't know much about functioning

out there in the real world

of ideas?

Yesterday

I talked with an old friend. She left teaching

to become a therapist. We sat in her car and she asked me,

are you talking to me as a friend or a therapist because I can't really be

your therapist.

It felt like a trick question. Like all of these questions I ask myself.

Light on a small pond makes me think

I am the center of the universe

like I have all of the advantages of floating in space,

not tied to anything,

but the shore is right there. Cattails,

nests in cattails, water iris, yellow

yellow water iris, carp rising to the top,

visible as fear.

It is possible to drown in a teaspoon of water

or choke on my own spit

when I bite into a plum so juicy I'm not ready

for that explosion in my mouth.

Small ponds are like small children,

they accept things as they are. There's always room for

    improvement, sure,

but I don't always want to work on that.

Do you feel shame? My friend asked me.

Of course I do

I said. But the light was ending

and I didn't want to have to drive home in the dark

by myself.

Postmodern Woman Bathing

Where does it say, in all the work we've read,
that we should float
>
> as Ophelia did,
>
> a mealy bar of soap,

our glycerin skin

> too soft for love those days on the ledge
>
> of a sink.

> And how were we to know
>
> that our young, obedient bodies would seem tragic,
>
> as Edna's did,

so small and fumbling, from shore?

> Virginia might have been our last great hope,

but even she sank quickly

> in the cold and shallow Ouse.

Her pockets storied stones.

I wonder

> as I straddle a porcelain tub

and strum the steaming water with my toe
what it's like to be immersed
then finished in a frothy senseless

> "ness." Still, it's here

in heat that stuns, I see

no easy end—

      a shot of rage
the chaser, glee, her lungs first fire
then stone.

STRAWBERRY PIE

In memory of Julia Wheeler, 1963-2000

It wasn't meant for me,
this tenderness
to which each berry succumbed:
small misshapen hearts she chose
not to taste since they might turn to acid
on her chemo-ed tongue. And
as mothers share their children, gratefully,
she offered pie I relished.

I thought, at first, I ate for her.
Grief's like that, vicarious and blue,
a heron hovering overhead
abstract as words and as awkward.
Our neighborhood refused to say it
—that she's dying
for a piece of strawberry pie.

Now I see I ate without knowing why,
except that what was offered me
was perfect, and was hers.

At The Feeder, Early November

At first it seems a mostly social situation,
the nuthatch clowning around upside down
on the post, a tufted titmouse
pretending to be somebody else,
looking, through the glass, like a mute cardinal
in that gray get up.

Hulls they litter to the breeze interminably,
I sweep. So I feed them bacon

raw, on a cracked "bird of paradise" plate,
its blue positioned so the wings are circling
its rim imperfect as memory,
Sunday breakfast,
nearly twelve. They are about as interested
as their painted mates and prove it
in perfect proportion to their plan:
if they feed us, we will come. We watch them as if
they were a religion we've invented.

Tomorrow is another day:

nothing to wake to but morning's dull-gray light;
hickories hold their own in thirty-mile-per-hour gusts.

The birds have disappeared.

For the hell of it I keep watch, remembering

some days we did not need to eat.

Some days it was all we could do to be nowhere

among the soldiering trees.

Birdhouse Gourds

They would be something to love,
to let take over
my otherwise uncertain heart.
Unworried they would climb the trellis
like clematis, though heavier,
leaves as large as Jack's giant's palm,
given the opportunity,
the time.

I recognize where my talents lie:
in wanting, in not pruning,
allowing the vine to stray;
I let them climb in their fairy tale
up the side of my house,
stretching onto the roof,
hanging down from the eaves,
holding on with shoots
that stick like a dream of someone
I barely remember.
They cut the tips of my fingers.
My thumbs.

This is a love story,
Jack descended. Acceptable
since harsher wars
have been.

After all, it is here on the ground

love finds itself

making a mess of things.

Inedible fruit.

Somewhere in there hangs a perfect home for martins.

Blue birds.

I just have to carve a little, gut

the thing. But carefully,

so the hole I am making into a doorway

will fit perfectly

the one who will stay.

LATE

I want a word for it, that glare the neighbor

from her kitchen window cannot hide.

A fence of leafy things makes no easy task, of wire

meant for something else,

rusted now and difficult to bend.

The dirt I work is nothing more than stone

beat down by miles and miles of rain

and petrified by hours. The "wedding veil?"

I dug it up. The neighbor moved away.

It's back again, perennial, and free.

Flashpoint

Your death is still an opening
through which we see the life left

in this world. What you took
from your sons and daughter

you gave back again through me.
Days I want more, I look at what you are:

three children who outlive
the burden of dumb hours.

I love you, then, that yours,
without your presence, leave me full,

a pail that you set down.

SUICIDES

1.

Tired of his options—
suicide, gun-running, divorce—
Terry Thompson unlocks the gate
to his private zoo enclosure,
releases the cats, the young macaque,
four grizzlies—
—all of his animals—
into the late afternoon light,
finally shooting himself in the head,
but not before
unfastening his wranglers
and taking out his junk, like presenting a gift
to his ex-wife the white tiger
will not refuse.

Over the ridge, his neighbor, Sam,
waits in the barn on his Pinto, Red. His mom,
Mrs. Kopchak, watches on WHIZ TV,
safe inside the house.

When the last lion steps into moonlight,
ghostly, spiritual-like, it's too late
to save the animals.

Even in the telling, redemption looks like

black fur on the rambling roses

the woods will not be rid of;

growls purr up from the dark, mine and

a middle-aged man's on a pony

just off I-70

who waited in the quiet for someone

to call the authorities to come

and kill every last beast.

2.

Some stories should be left alone,

like why a decent man like you

would kill himself. Or why

a nut-case might keep 48 exotic animals in cages

on his 40-acre farm

only to release them on a late October afternoon

before pulling down his Wranglers, taking out his junk,

and shooting himself in the head.

Some stories should be left alone

because there is no way to defend them

and no way not to see ourselves

in the darkest versions of others.

Why we might want to die

as the farm's tall grass gives way to frost,

why the blue of the sky is a Parrish blue

so that a painter tries harder to forgive himself.

As if to share the pain is to halve it.

An animal run wild, coaxed to light.

3.

Maybe I shouldn't care so much about the details

  of *this* suicide

  since I didn't know him

except by association since he lived just a few miles

from my new boyfriend who wouldn't even be

my new boyfriend

  if *you* hadn't also committed suicide,

and hearing about his exotic farm

and his former gun-running and recent divorce

  made me think I better know what I'm getting myself into.

  Like, are all men from *that* county this nuts?

And, will I be with this new guy for 11 years and one day

    find a note explaining the unexplainable

    stashed under the driver seat of my Kia Rio?

  Will he find his options narrowing like the light

as night falls off I-70 on a hillside

strewn with the carcasses of 47 un-domesticated animals?

A big cat recognizes fear when he smells it.

Even born in a cage,
       a man craves freedom

       lets them all out—
the big cats, a small macaque, the grizzly—
       one day falling to dusk in October, 2011,
       the details on t.v.
       He shot himself in the head.
       How you did it.

Do details matter when everything goes dark?

Sixteen days it took me to find your note
       at the car wash in my peach dress.
I was reaching beneath my driver's seat
when I found the indecipherable notes you had written
as if scribbling in the dark.

Leaving The Old House

1. The Grave

I don't think love dies with the body
shot in the mouth and burned to ash and
buried in a pine box on the hill above *Helber's Church*,
George and Isabelle painted on the transom,
our children digging for crawdads in the culvert
on the day we put you underground, the grave
squared off, plotted out, reserved,
my cursive *J* entwined with your *D*
making its way among the wild pea vine.

2. The End

Beyond the bed stripped clean,
sheets pulled from corners,
pillows tossed like bombs to the floor,
out in the dark, through the glass
lies The Queen in her Chair,
the outline of a woman

black between her legs and arms and crown
the only sound, a dryer tumbling,
a full heart, nothing like a constellation
where we keep our better selves
for wishing upon.

3. Leaving the Old House

It's not the mice, the girl
an easy catch, her eyes perpetual in
What? Or her mate

inclined to take the meal and run,
the trap flipped empty,
his tiny rifle fire to show he'd won.

It's not dreams of other men
I'd never do in life. The distant squirrels
who chew the wires inside my sleepy head.

Not morning sun that has no way inside
but through the cracks in shutters drawn,
tree branches, holes of shadow on the wall.

It's not regret that someone tried,
what anchored us to discipline and dream.
It's that you chose against kissing
this place goodbye. It's that you stay.
It's that you never thought
I might want something else, some kind of peace.
The thing you did in spite of truth:
the left-hand faucet cold the right-hand, warm,
backwards, fool.

Wanting You

Because without you
in the flesh, you are a quirk of mine,

a line I continually cross,
except it is March,

and the rain holds everything close
the exhaled cigarette,

the animal's wet fur,
the smell clinging.

Stupidly I sit at the edge
of some threshold. That urge

to forget. That nothing.
You glide into abstraction

like a comet, a heavenly body,
through yesterday's black condition.

Circe's Lament

After "The Inarticulate," Michael Waters

I.

I meant to brush him off,
sand from my thigh.
But his ship teased the horizon,
so I lied
that my magic didn't matter,
that I could sleep forever in his arms.
The slippery slope of knowing
he felt nothing left me crushing rue
that stunk of swine.

I could have told the truth and cried.
I would have served him every cup.
I could have let him drink me like a cure.
Dress me like a doll.
Stone me on the street.
Know me like a whore.

I would have been the scar
he carries on his thigh,
that boar who took a piece and left
its beauty mark.

II.

I'd be myself again.
You'd think a siren's beauty wouldn't fade.
Time shrinks me to a shrew
while history rides a girl
who wets herself and combs the sand for perfect
pinkish shells. He wears them like a talisman,
strung about his wrinkled neck three times.

We tossed about like ships
that crest and crest and never break,
all foam and salt, a ruined cup come time to drink.
I tried to rest. I let him sleep for years.

Docile. Wild. No difference here.
Silence. Song. I can not care.
It's never been more clear.

III.

Touching your scar, I am like a wife
who worries for nothing, the damage done, the wound's beauty
growing as mine fades into thinning nails and hair and lines
    drawn here,

along my philtrum's cup, where Ugly maps itself without consent,
and Courage proves itself along your thigh.
In dreams you know the sorceress

who reaches with her sooty, boar's-tusk wand
and now you see my deepest thoughts.
The ones I would not share.

Listen to your stupid snore! The saddest, most pathetic sound!
You breathe under water. I swim in air
and think your sleep is like the prow of some great ship

arranging how we part. *Forever* is a word no mortal speaks.
Not even you who know how long it seems,
swept up in *this*, alive, but always half asleep.

Touching your scar, I am like a wife
brought back to wits with a slap, the sting
momentary, bright, articulate.

According To The Old Farmer's Almanac, January 13, 2003, Is Plough Monday

You say you're sorry.
Sorry like the wind's sorry.
Or the skin where the splinter's been.
Because whatever happens, happens
to you. You're a case of mistaken
identity, nobody's cat leaping
through the cyclamen. The moon
a full wolf. Time for pruning—
again, not your fault. A natural
phenomenon and the mother
of diligence. Everything
epiphany. Tradition says
this is the coldest day of the year.
Don't get lost in the calendar
waiting for spring. At least you live
in the present as a twelve-year-old
is required, the only thing you do
that's required. I hated you today
for thirty-two seconds. The buds
blast, drying up before they open,
Gardenia, my difficult flower.

CALENDULA

from the Latin meaning "little calendar"

"Little clock," little "weather glass,"
pot marigold, "referring to the Virgin
Mary," unnatural bloom of December,
goes to seed one stalk at a time, as if marking time
were the main business of a flower:

clinching its little fists,
refusing at first to let go,
each soul carcass dark,
microscopically ridged, curled
like the fingernail of the dead
child that it might deliver
the passage of time, this time,
less vainly, more rivetingly, or
reinventing itself, self-seeding
this particularly orange morning

taking care not to brown or burn
at dawn in the fallen frost.

Third time this year it's made the rounds,
seed to stalk to flower and back to seed,
redundant as self love, but different:

—day 261 of living

since

that inevitable turn

for the worse—then

the present tense of a perfect, orange flower—

this one, whose petals skirt a little,

turning itself

on.

Everything Depends Upon

sex and how well we position ourselves,

the elbow developing a wing,

the reciprocating knee,

the bird at the window proving

all ledges are not for jumping—

sometimes perching, watching with great admiration

how a foot can be a part when it is nothing more than bone

and sometimes broken, what

I love about you is your body, how it moves

around your soul, a hand inside a glove, and when I see it bare

like this and wanting, I think how honey wants the bee

to come.

Reading By Streetlamp On Governor Ave.

Because it's hard to love, the streetlamp hums.
Because it's hard to see, all those beautiful bugs
beating with their bodies the light back in,

a bat's attracted.
He feels. He feeds.
And light would be light, could he see.

How smart, though,
to feel the lamppost without touching it?
Is it that it's warm beforehand?

But then, having been felt,
scanned up and down, not touched—
how this touches me now—

on my sectional couch in broad book-light.
How does it feel to be tumbling back
to the cirri incurious bat

into whose shape?
So he skeets up, edging to the left
to meet the ingenuous flutter,
his blind date. How does it feel
to be love flirting back?
That shape.

Sitting Centerfield On The Night Game Of Your Suicide

Tonight, no stars, just miles turning

to light years before our eyes: You, on the mound

gesturing home, who cock your head

and flash that crooked grin. Then,

bizarre news: small dogs thrown from speeding cars;

flag-less moons; rhinoceros bones

that come unglued

from dinosaur lies; and

still, devotees, here we are, in our own conspiracy,

caps on tight, hot dog night,

feigning happiness in the bleeder seats.

We know the frivolity of throwing up a glove,

the hollowness of a bad call.

The vanity of trying to run.

Widow Of A Modern-Day Icarus

Right away she took a lover,
skin like silt,
same frame (too heavy to float)
same perfect fit in the sack.

Afterward, she'd drive home through the dark,
console lit blue, smoke
his imported cigarettes, leave him
to sleep to mend his back,

imagine herself
falling
from the bridge between Minneapolis
and St. Paul, leaving
no proof of her
crime, her small indulgences.
Purposeful. Had she truly existed,

she would have misspelled Aegean, secretly
corrected his drawl,
planted viny things on his grave, desired

many, many men since many

smell of axle grease and too much sun
and own a family dog.

The Onion

I want to love it for what it is,
the burn I bite into,
the taste in the tuna, what saves me
from ever being merely
satisfied.

I want to peel the paper layer,
cut out the hairy heart
and take it like an apple
to my mouth.

It sits in my stomach,
a stone in the disposal of my discontent.
Flicks my brain
with the faintest idea.

What can I do but disguise it,
sprinkle it
fine as salt
on the wound of desire?

Potamophobia (At A Stadium On The Ohio River)

I don't love this river, same as I don't

love this game, the middle

lull, innings four through six,

when the jerky, syncopated rag I was beginning

to settle into

suddenly stops—midstream,

measures of idleness I could steer

a barge through—and it dawns on me

I'm afraid that this boredom

is actually the stillness

pretending to be a dark mirror.

I learn to pay attention. Foul balls

hit their mark, fans who've lost focus,

and Bench gestures telepathic

calls, while the batter stands ready

(he thinks) for something significant

and tragic as love across the Moors.

Who can know? It's like Algebra in French

or shoveling coal in a tug boat.

God loves

feigning pity, so She invented

the seventh inning stretch, to prepare me,

I guess, for game's end, to get my blood
to fill my lungs with a song that begs
to be "taken out" when I'm already there,
makes me shake off the sun and stand
completely erect,
because it's going to start now,
the excitement; This is it. We
are preparing for the end.

Trees cast their lines, bad calls, frayed ends,
as we coast downriver, rapids
around the bend; the relief
pitcher steps onto the mound,
and though the whole stadium
hangs on his first pitch,
I imagine he's going to balk,
chancing a pickoff at first.
So what if he throws a strike?

Here in the stands
of Riverfront Stadium,
on the far side
of seven, starting to trust, I
learn fear, unannounced.
It's Borbon for god's sake;
who else
could I want? Still,

so much I don't get: the shame

I've known of residual doubt,

even Christ earned it,

his first step out,

such murky water,

a dozen men heckling as they place their bets.

Then, someone close by

starts to chant, the organ chords

building a ramp to the arc

of laughter. I'm learning

it's okay to join, small

as I am, ignorant,

and completely off pitch.

Conversation With Two-Time Mid-American Conference Relief Pitcher Douglas Dean Stackhouse On Winning, Losing, And Learning To Fiddle

> *There is a change—and I am poor;*
> *Your love hath been, nor long ago,*
> *A fountain at my fond heart's door,*
> *Whose only business was to flow;*
> *And flow it did; not taking heed*
> *Of its own bounty, or my need.*
> —William Wordsworth

"Taking up the fiddle at 50" I
toss to the wind,

    like a bad call on a perfect pitch,

"would be like your trying to throw again."

I had thought the rotting zinnias clung to a memory
of success. I point out a jar of them

        propped in the window.

"There is no going back," he says, throws his gear

    over his shoulder,

        and leaves

      another glimmering testament:

"When I won, it was no big deal.

    I was supposed to win," he says.

But when I lost,

          we lost. I couldn't go back and change it."

I take lessons, play the scales back,

     let the freshly dead (notes, petals, words)
          confetti the kitchen floor.

I imagine, in September, the jar in the window

                    blushing with flowers,

and tolerate the dog's rebuke.

     Then I consider the solitary act
     of so much bowing, as
strings ignite the sweet spot;

the burled neck, the smooth stroke,
and the cool relief of "Stack"
     pitching out of the stretch:

"This is not Macbeth," says teacher Liz, "We are not witches
stirring a pot!"

     and she ruins me with an LP of Tommy Jarrel's "Cripple
Creek."

     What can I do but separate the cream

from all of that churning:

      winding up a pitch;

throwing a cutter,

     culling seeds from finished stalks;

     riding a Ferris wheel in the dark...what

but trade blind hope—

       for an alley cat's complaint—

and keep listening to the masters.

Camellia

In the back corner of the yard against the fence
where the sun can't find you,
the mulberry hogging it all,
you try to flower.

Pink as pretty as your name
doesn't last, not even
the shade grass he planted,
not the half-dug fish pond,
my young bamboo.
All names for you, japonica,
are difficult in shadow.

Still, you swing a little
when the rabbit hides between your wiry cage.
You seem to try
a little harder now that I've trimmed,
and dragged, and prayed.
You disguise my willingness to fail,
afire in the pit, not meant to flame,
though you do, with your pink
underside of things.

I think about transplanting you.
But you're much too big,

the ground too hard. *Beautiful*

might mean *No*. Or, *I'll show you next time*

how to live.

My Icarus

1.

I can't imagine falling through weightless clouds
the way a heavy breast falls from a wired cup;
a gimpy foot falls with each deliberate, uneven step;
the way a car glides over a cliff in an ending you want to forget,
the story good except for that.

I meant to hold you more.
Please, imagine that I did. Consider how
not holding you
allowed the weight of my grief
to take me
to wherever it is you went.

2.

Home is a sky for lumbering birds.
All that blue makes you confess
and you become what you are
without thinking. Without even trying.

3.

 Gulls storm the ledges: *Don't get too close*
to what you want.
I know, I know.
You try and then forget.
I think everyone who matters forgets.
A wife
would have loved you most
as she watched you falling,
and a sister would have
painted your name on the whitewash of her boat.
That and wings. Plus
a devil's tail anchor. She would have understood
your paradox.

4.

We can only imagine what you wanted,
what you saw of us on the ground, waving frantically,
happy at first you were flying,
then swimming out to find you in the brilliant surf.

ABOUT THE AUTHOR

Jane Ann (Devol) Fuller's poetry has appeared in *Aethlon, Atticus Review, B O D Y, Denver Quarterly, Fifth Wednesday, Grist, JMWW, Kamana, Northern Appalachia Review, Pine Mountain Sand and Gravel, Pudding Magazine, Rise Up Review, Shenandoah, Steinbeck Now, Still: the Journal, Sugar House Review, The American Journal of Poetry, The Ekphrastic Review, The MacGuffin, The Pikeville Review,* and *Waccamaw.*

Fuller's work appears in the anthologies *All We Know of Pleasure: Poetic Erotica by Women,* edited by Enid Shomer, *Project Hope: The Center for Victims of Torture,* edited by Betsy Brown, and *Women of Appalachia Project,* edited by Kari Gunter-Seymour.

Fuller is a recipient of the James Boatwright III Poetry Prize. She co-authored *Revenants: A Story of Many Lives,* published with a grant from the Ohio Arts Council. She studied English Literature at Ohio University and earned her MFA from the Iowa Writer's Workshop. She lives in the Hocking Hills of southeastern Ohio.

Sheila-Na-Gig Editions